Round about Our Coal Fire,

or,

Christmas Entertainments

Wherein it is Described,

TOGETHER WITH

Some Curious Memoirs of Old Father *Christmas*; Shewing What, Hospitality Was in Former Times, and How Little There Remains of it at Pretent.

Illustrated with Many Diverting Cuts

London
Spradabach Publishing
2024

SPRADABACH PUBLISHING
BM Box Spradabach
London WC1N 3XX

Round Our Coal Fire, or, Christmas Entertainments

First published in 1734
First Spradabach edition published 2024
© Spradabach Publishing 2024

Interior design by Alex Kurtagic

ISBN 978-1-909606-55-5

British Library Cataloguing-in-Publication Data:
A catalogue record for this book is available from the British Library.

To the

Worshipful Mr. LUN,

Complete Witch-Maker of England, and Conjurer General of the Universe, at His Great House in Covent Garden.

SIR,

Though I have read Dr. Glanville of Witches, and is very plain to me, that none of the Writers on these Matters ever had half the Witchcraft in them which you possess or ever could produce such agreeable Devils and Witches as you have daily introduced.

I have Witneses enough to assert my Conjecture; for my Cousin *Sarah*, Cousin *Dolly*, Cousin *Nancy*, and a Score more of them, when any Stories are told of *Witches*, *Hobgoblins*, *Bull-Beggars*, *Raw-Heads* and *Bloody-Bones*, *Ghosts*, &c. will crowd together into a Bed, in a hot Summer's Night, and sweat to such a degree as if they had taken a Pound of *Venice* Treacle; so great is the Fear they are possessed with when they hear the lamentable Stories handed down to them by their Great Grandmothers: But when Mr. *Lunn* bad occasionally invented a new Devil, or a Legion or two of Witches, there was no rest in the House till they were decked out, and managed the Tack so as to get a fair Sight of them: although the Night proved never so dark, they always came home Gay, and could lie single in Bed; which renders it plain to me, that your Magick far excels what the old Folks used to relate of Friar *Bacon*, and the Sorcerers in the Days of Yore. The old ones played their own Game with the Boys and Girls in their Times, who never could go to Bed without the Shelter of a Pillow; but who the Devil would not rob an Orchard to see the Devils of your making.

But pray Mr LUN, are not your Devils Men? I do assure you if they are, some Ladies of my Acquaintance are prodigiously fond of them; and if they should really prove Ghosts or Spirits, they are resolved to run heading to the Devil for them. See then

the Difference between my Grandmother's Devils
and your Devils.

So I conclude,

Your's, &c.

DICK MERRYMAN.

Table of Contents

Note on This Edition

he text in this volume is based on the illustrated fourth edition, 'with great additions', of *Round about our Coal Fire, or, Christmas Entertainments*, published in London by J. Roberts, and first published in 1734. It is reproduced in its entirety.

The capitalisation and punctuation appear as in the original, except in the chapter titles and title page; as do the italics, except for quoted poetry and proverbs, which appeared an in italics and have been set in roman type.

Prologue

I.

You merry, merry Souls,
    Christmas is a coming,
We shall have flowing Bowls,
Dancing, piping, drumming.

II.

Delicate Minced Pies,
   To feast every Virgin.
Capes and Goose likewise,
   Brawn, and a Dish of Sturgeon.

III.

Then for your Christmas Box,
   Sweet Plum Cakes and Money,
Delicate Holland Smocks,
   Kisses sweet as Honey.

IV.

Hey for the Christmas Ball,
   Where we shall be jolly,
Coupling short and tall,
   Kate, Dick, Ralph, and Molly.

V.

Then to the hop we'll go,
   Where we'll jig and caper,
Cuckolds all-a-row,
   Will shall pay the Scraper.

VI.

Hodge ball dance with Prue,
   Keeping Time with Kisses;
We'll have a jovial Crew,
   Of sweet Smirking Misses.

CHAPTER I

The Mirth and Jollity of the Christmas Holidays; *viz.* Christmas Gambols, Eating, Drinking, Kissing, and other Diversions.

irst acknowledging the sacredness of the Holy Time of Christmas, I proceed to set forth the Rejoicing which are generally made at that great Festival.

You must understand, good People, that the Manner of celebrating this great Course of Holydays, is vastly different now to what it was in former Days: There was once upon a Time Hospitality in the Land; an *English* Gentleman at the opening of the great Day, had all his Tenants and Neighbours enter'd his Hall by Day-break, the strong Beer was broach'd, and the Black-Jacks went plentifully about with Toast, Sugar, Nutmeg, and good Cheshire Cheese; the Rooms were embower'd with Holly, Ivy, Cypress, Bays, Laurel, and Missleto, and a bouncing *Christmas* Log in the Chimney, glowing like the Cheeks of a Country Milk-maid; then was the Pewter as bright as *Clarinda*, and every bit of Brass as polished as the most refined Gentleman, the Servants were then running here and there with merry Hearts and jolly Countenances; every one was busy in welcoming of Guests, and look'd as smug as new lick'd Puppies; the Lasses were as blithe and buxom as the Maids in good Queen Bess's Days, when they eat Sir Loins of Roast Beef for Breakfast; *Peg* would scuttle about to make a Toast for *John*, while *Tom* ran *harum scarum* to draw a Jug of Ale for *Margery*: Gaffer *Spriggins* was bid thrice welcome by the Squire, and Goody *Goose* did not fail of a smacking Buss from his Worship in memory of past Favours, while his Son and Heir was mousling and tousling the blooming Beautes of the Tenant's Daughters: In a Word, the Spirit of Generosity ran through the whole House.

In these Times all the Spits were sparkling, the *Hackin* must be boiled by Day-break, or else two young Men took the Maiden by the Arms, and run her round the Market Place, till the was ashamed of her Laziness. And what was worse than this, she must not play with the young Fellows that Day, but stand neuter, like a Girl in a Winding-sheet at a Church door for a Bastard Child.

But now let us enquire a little farther, to arrive at the Sense of the Thing; this great Festival was in former Times kept with to much that every one in the freedom and Openness of Heart, that every one in the country where a gentleman resided, possessed at least a day of pleasure in the *Christmas* holidays; the tables were all spread from the first to the last, the sirloins of beef, the minc'd pies, the plum porridge, the capons, turkies, geese, and plum puddings, were all brought upon the board; and all those who had sharp stomachs and sharp knives eat heartily and were welcome, which gave rise to the Proverb,

Merry in the Hall, when beards wag all.

There were then Turnspits employed, who by the Time Dinner was over, would look as Black and as greasy as a Welch Porridge Pot, but the Jacks have since turned them all out of Doors. The Geese which used to be fattened for the honest Neighbours, have been of late sent to London, and the Quills made into Pens to convey away the Landlord's Estate; the Sheep are drove away to raise Money to answer the Loss at a Game at Dice or Cards, and their Skins made into Parchment for

Deeds and Indentures; nay, even the poor innocent Bee, who used to pay its Tribute to the Lord once a Year, at least, in good Metheglin, for the Entertainment of the Guests, and its Wax converted into beneficial Plaisters for sick Neigh bours, is now used for the sealing of Deeds to his Disadvantage.

But give me the Man *who has a good Heart in his Belly*, and has Spirit enough to keep up the old Way of Hospitality, feeds his People till they are as plume as Partridges, and as far as Porpoises, that every Servant may appear as jolly as the late Bishop of *Winchester*'s Porter at *Chelsea* and now keep a Parcel of sneeking looking Wretches about them, whose Ribs a was apparent as those of a Gridiron. What an honour it is to a Master to hear the Folks about him praise his Generosity! And such a Character is a help to him sometimes at an Election; for Servants who are kept under a good natured Direction must love their Master and make the Country Folks admire him more from their Praises of him, for there is always one or other of them setting forth his Goodnesss; it makes a greater Impression on those who never saw him, or ever had been at his House.

When I speak this, I recollect the Fable of the Mouse, who helped the Lion out of the Toil he was caught in, and likewise the common Opinion, that a Mouse may destroy an Elephant; besides another Observation, that a Mouse may creep where an Elephant cannot go, and do good when some People least expect it."

Then let all your Folks live briskly, and at such a Time of Rejoicing, enjoy the Benefit of good Beef and Pudding, let the strong Beer be unlocked, and let the Piper play,

O'er the Hills and far away.

And also,

Strike up Drowsy-gut Scrapers,
Gallants be ready,
Each with his Lady, &c.

For there must be a Dance now then by way of Exercise and Wit, or else I am sure *Hurlo Thrumbo* was in the wrong Box, as well as the old Ballad Woman, who gave you a Song and a Dance, and all for the Price of a Half-penny.

I have now by me two Squires and a Sir—— who say I am mad to write in this manner, for they are jealous I hint at them. One says to me, when did you ever find me stingy, I believe you have a Mind to reflect on my Character. A second says, "when did I make away my Estate by my Goose Quills, the Parchment from my Sheeps Backs, and the Wax of my Bees?" And says the third, "And pray, Sir, how can you censure me on any account? Have not I treated you with many Bottles of Claret? And did not I laugh as loud as any one when we were at *Hurlo Thrumbo* together?" And then I dropped my Subject, as many noted Preachers do, and sum'd up the Matter in few Words, *viz.*

> Gentlemen,
> If I have told you of your Sins, mend if you can for the future, let the Stingy be Generous, let the Generous be Wise, and let him who is between one and the other keep his Claret to himself if he will, and laugh less, when there is nothing to be laughed at.

Butthen it is said,

> Laugh and be Fat——————

Which Words may be understood thus if a Man has but a mean Subsistence, he can never have any great occasion to Laugh, and much less to be Fat; but if he has Plenty of Provender, then the Proverb is right, *He may laugh that wins*, and be Fat into-the Bargain.

The News-Papers, however, informs us, that the Spirit of Hospitality has not quite forsaken us; for three or four of them tell, that several of the Gentry are gone down to their Seats in the Country, in order to keep their Christmas in the old Way, and entertain their Tenants and Trades folks as their Ancestors used to do, and I wish them a merry Christmas accordingly. I must also take notice to the stingy Tribe, that if they don't at least make their Tenants or Tradesmen drink when they come to see them in the *Christmas* Holidays, they have Liberty of pissing behind the Door, which is a Law of very ancient Date.

A merry Gentleman of my Acquaintance desires I will insert, that the old Folks in Days of yore kept open House at *Christmas* out of Interest; for then says he they received the greatest Part of their Rent in Kind; such as Wheat, Barley or Malt, Oxen, Calves, Sheep, Swine, Turkies, Capons, Geese, and suchlike; and they not having Room enough to preserve their Grain, or Fodder enough to sustain their Cattle or Poultry, nor Markets to fell off the Overplus, they were obliged to use them in their own House and by treating the People of the County, gained Credit amongst them, and riveted the Minds and Good-will of their Neighbours to firmly in them, that no one dare venture to oppose them. The Squire's Will was done what ever came on it; for if he happened to ask a Neighbour what it was o'clock, they returned with a low Scrape, It is what your Worthip pleases.

The Dancing and Singing of the Benchers in the great Inns of Court in *Christmas*, is in some sort founded upon Interest; for they hold, as I am informed, some Privilege by, Dancing about the Fire in the Middle of their Hall, and singing the Song of *Round about our Coal Fire*, &c.

This Time of Year being cold and frosty generally Speaking, or when Jack Frost commonly takes us by the Nose, the Diversions are within Doors, either in Exercise or by the Fire Side.

Country-Dancing is one of the chief Exercises: *Moll Peaty* and the *Black Joke* are never forgot;

these Dances stir the Blood, and give the Males and Females a fellow feeling of each others Activity, Ability, and Agility; Cupid always sits in the Corner of the Room where these Diversions are transacting, and shoots Quivers full of Arrows at the Dancers, and makes his own Game of them.

Then comes Mumming or Masquerading, when the 'Squire's Wardrobe is ransacked for Dresses of all Kinds, and the Coal-hole searched around, or Corks burnt to black the Faces of the Fair, or make Deputy Mustaches, and every one in the Family, except the 'Squire himself must be transformed from what they were; then begins the Freedom between one and the other to be sprinkled about the Hall, and every one shews their Wit according to their Capacity, and then a Dance again, and a good hearty Pull or two at Silver Tankard of Strong Beer, made woundy good with Sugar and Nutmeg. Then *Jenny* gives you a Jig, which is proportionably good as it makes her abound in Sweat; *Doll*, in her way, gives you a Double-Courant, and turns round fifty times in a Minute, till most of them are drunk enough, and reel home, or lie down in the Barn.

Or else there is a Match at *Blind-Man's-Buff*, and then it is lawful to set any thing in the way for Folks to tumble over, whether it be to break Arms, Legs, or Heads, 'tis no matter, for Neck-or-nothing, the Devil loves no Cripples.—This Play, I am told, was first set on foot by the Country Bone-setters, who like some Surgeons, when they first set up Business in the Country, provide two or three

pickled Whores of Figure to P—x the Parish; both
very necessary Steps towards gaining good Business.

As for *Puss in the Corner*, that is a very harm-
less Sport, and one may ramp at it as much as one
will; for at this Game when a Man catches a Woman, he may kiss her till her Ears crack, or she will
be disappointed if she is a Woman of any Spirit;
but if it is one who offers at a Struggle and blush-
es, then be assured she is a Prude, and though she
won't stand a Buss in Public, the will receive it with
open Arms behind the Door, and you may kiss her
till the makes your Heart ake.

The next Game to this is *Questions and Commands*, when the Commander may oblige his
Subject to answer any lawful Question, and make
the same obey him instantly, under the Penalty of
being founded, or paying such Forfeit as may be
laid on the Agressor; but the Forfeits being generally fixed at some certain Price, as a Shilling,
Half a Crown, &c. so every one knowing what to
do if they should be too stuborn to submit, make
themselves easy at discretion. At one of these Entertainments, I remember a Gentleman was com-
manded to take a certain Lady into the next Room,
and make her squsak; he took the Lady according
to Order; and was free enough in a modest way,
But, Madam, says he, why don't you squeak? Sir,
answered the Lady, you are to make me squeak:
But, returns the Gentleman, if you don't squeak,
I must forfeit: Why don't you make me says the

Lady: And though there was a Couch in the Room, and he was put to the last Push, she would not squeak, and the poor Gentleman was forced to pay the Forfeit after he had taken so much pains with her. Some would have made him lay down double the Money, *i. e.* one Part as a Fordeit, and the other for Socket-money.

As for the Game of *Hoop and Hide*, the Parties have the Liberty of hiding where they will, in any Part of the House; and if it should prove to be in a Bed, and if they even then happen to be caught, the Dispute ends in Kissing, &c.

Most of the other Diversions are Cards and Dice, but they are seldom set on foot, unless a Lawyer is at hand, to breed some Dispute for him to decide, or at least have some Party in.

And now I come to another Entertainment frequently used, which is of the Story-telling Order, *viz.* of Hobgoblins, Witches, Conjurers, Ghosts, Fairies, and such like common Disturbers.

CHAPTER II

Treating of Hobgoblins, Raw-Heads and Bloody-Bones, Buggy Bows, Tom Pokers, Bull-Beggars; and Such Like Horrible Bodies.

There was nothing kept me in greater Awe when I was a Child, than the frequent Relations I had from my Grandmother and nurse, of Hobgoblins and Bull-beggers; they would tell me such Stories of them daily, as would frighten me into a woeful Case, and sad Disgrace, and then

11

I was surely disciplined by the Rod, and if I cried only at the terrible Apprehensions I had imbibed of such Monsters, I was whipped for crying, and whipped again for crying when I was whipped, so that I lived a sad Life: I was daily fed with Terrors, and as duly chastised for swallowing them; then I was as certainly flogged if I told what was called a Lie; for if I happened only to ask my Grandmother whether there was such a horrible Thing as told me of "What Sirrah (says she) do you scruple I tell you, for Truth? You tell a Lie in your Thoughts whilst you suspect my Truth." And then I was whipped again for that; and so I had my Chastisement for every thing almost I did, through my Nurse or Grandmother's Narrations: And truly till I was arrived at Man's Estate, I could hardly part with the Apprehensions of Hobgoblins when I was in the Dark; so sympatick a Power had the Rod communicated to the Brain by the way of my Backside. But since I am arrived at Years of Discretion to know what they are, I discovered them to be of the Human Race; one a poor starved snarlig Critic, another a Man who had Impudence enough to pyrate the Works of other Men , a third who valued himelf more for his Guts than his Brains, and could only say Bo!—Another a little squirting fellow, who aimed at being a Flea in a Man's Ear; another a Bite and Scandal-bearer, and so on.

Such Cabals as I speak of are in many Corners of the Earth, and in full Club make their Chairman pronounce the Doom of all before them; therefore such as these should not any longer appear as Bug Bears either to Men, Women, or Children, for when we know them the Enchantment is broke, and their Gang perishes. Yet as a great Man says, in his Preface to an Account of Denmark, "The Prejudice of Education is hardly to be overcome 'till our Age is incapable of admitting our own Reason to act for itfelf." But be this as it will, let us see what use the Country Folks make of Hobgoblins, Raw-Heads and Bloody-Bones, &c.

When they are tired with Dancing and Romps, they take their Places about the Fire; Alack, (says *Nan*) have you not heard of the Bull-Beggar in the fall Close by our House, that straddles along every Night as soon as it is dark? I am sure my Mother has seen it may a Night, for the has told me so over and over, and I am afraid to go home alone after it is dark. Nay (says *John*) I shall see you safe home, for that Close is a famous Place for Bull-Beggars; your Mother is in the right on't, for the used to walk out there herself o' Nights; and I have seen a tall Thing in white, in the Shape of a tall Man, throw her down under a Hay-Rick. But, my dear *Nan*, I will protect you from such a Devil; if you should be frightened at any Thing you should see, I will take you to the other Corner, and give you the Staff of Knowledge which will make you as good a Woman and as wide your Mother. Alack, says *Mary*, my Fingers itch to see a Raw-Head and Bloody-Bones, for when Gaffer *Grey-Beard* was coming, to be sure I was dent to bed, and my Mother set up praying and fighting for four Hours afterwards; and if I have staid out a little more than ordinary at Market, then I knocked at the Door, my mother after a great deal of Fuss used to call us, Who's there—— Who's there—— and there I must say, though it was never so cold, till the *Hurry-com-Clutter* was over, and Gaffer *Grey-Beard* was conjured into the Oven; and this I know very well, for I saw a Cloven Foot, and heard a Voice cry-out Bo — Bo — Bo — just as I was going to warm myself; but my Mother in a violent Passion cried out, Hussey, go to bed, and rest there, you idle Slut; is it fit for you to keep your poor Mother out of Bed waiting for you to till this time of the Night: Go to Bed, I say, and leave me to bar the Doors; And so I did, but could not help peeping, and there was *John* killing my Mother as if Heaven and Earth were coming together; and to be sure there was a good roast Fowl taken out of the Cupboard, and a Tankard of Strong Beer; which made me remember the old Proverb, *To Bed with the Children, and lay the Goose to the Fire*, Lud! had I been in my Mother's. Place, I know what I know.——What do you think, says *Thomas*, if I see you safe home, and sit by you Bed-side all the Night; I can get in at the Window, and we with talk a little farther about Gaffer *Grey Beard*. Aye, dear *Thomas*, says the, I pray you see me safe home, for I fear I should be in a quaking Case if Gaffer should come.

Well now, says *Susan*, you may say what you will about these Hobgoblins and Things; but I can assure you, the Ragged Colt that walks in our Lane after Dark-light, keeps us all at home out of Fear, except my Sister *Sally*, and she, I believe, deals with the Devil; for the Sight of such a Bugbear would frighten us all out of our Wits: There is *Sally* we go out of sight's, let them be never so dark, with a Book in her Hand, an come home as pert as a Pearmonger; but the is a bold Girl, and will *resist anything, let what will come against her she will give them as good as they bring.* Why then, says *Roger*, I am your Man; and let the Ragged Colt be as big as *Powls* Steeple, I will swinge his jacket for him: Zouks, Girl, I will see thee safe, fear nothing when you hug honest Roger; and *if the Ragged Colt comes cling close about him, for have got a Conjuring Wand.* Ave, says *Susan*, and I know what that is; for a Master that I lived with some time ago almost conjured me out of my Senses, I am sure many a Night has he made me shake and quake in my Bed; but I soon found out his conjuring Tricks, and he is a vile perjured Wretch he deserves to go to the Gallows for his Sins; if I had then Pounds in the World I would hang him, if there was never another Man in *England*; a Brute, a Rogue, a Villain! I would conjure him to the Devil if I could meet with him.

Deary me, lays Mother *Wagstaff*, thou art but a Child still, and to pretend to talk of Conjuring-Wands at this Rate; correct the Passion, and

I will bring thee to be Mistress of a good House: You and I will go home together and talk about it, for I know who have and who have not Conjuring Wands in our Country, and you shall know the Secret.

It is very true, says Stephen, for there are Conjuring Wands enough with us; and if any one, can tell you the Secret, it is Mother *Wagstaff*; for my Lady asked her today about a ream, and the answered her main well. But, says *Peg*, though I have heard of Bull-beggars that frighten Folks, my Father says, that a Bailiff is a Bull-Beggar that frightens him the most, except it is Lawyer *Blunt*.

Truly, says *Roger*, I think our Parson is as great a Bull-Beggar as any at all; for I have heard him many a time fending Folks to the Devil: And then our Lawyer is as bad; for he first plagues a Man out of his Estate, and then makes him hang himself, or else makes him sick, and our Doctor kills him with Physick.

So, Gentlemen, here ends my Account of the Hobgoblin Society.

CHAPTER III

Of Witches, Wizards, Conjurers, and Such Trifles; What They Are, and How to Make Them; with Many of Their Merry Pranks, &c.

Among the other amusing Stories told in the Holiday Times, those of Witches, and their Pranks are not the least considerable. A Witch, according to Nurse's Account must be a hagged old Woman, living in a little rotten Cottage, under a Hill, by a Wood Side, and found frequently

17

spinning at the Door; she must have a black Cat, two or three Broomsticks, an Imp or two, and two or three Diabolical Teats to suckle her Imps. And then again, a Witch must be of so dry a Nature, that if you fling her into a River she will not sink; so hard then is her fate, that when she undergoes the Trial, if he does not drown, she must be burnt, as many have been in the Memory of Man.

The Male Witches are called Wizards or Conjurers; we have many Instances of them, such as Dr.*Faustus*, Friar *Bacon*, Mr. *Lun*, Dr. *Partridge*, seventh Sons, and Gentlemen who have the Second-sight, besides deaf and dumb Folks, &c.

But let these Sorcerers be of which Sex they will, they are generally said to possess the Gift of Enchantment, and can transform themselves into various Shapes whenever they will; as Cats, Hares, ragged Colts, or Bears, to the great Disturbance of the good People where ever they live.

As for those of the Female sort, as my Nurse told me, (for I must give you her account first) there was one Gammar *Martyn*, who lived at the End of the Town, where he was born; a sour-looking Woman, with an old high crowned Hat, a Broomstick generally in her Hand when the walked to Market, where she seldom bought any thing but Sheeps Lights, or such like Cats Meat, and the Folks wondered how the Devil the lived; the Boys used to call her Old Mother Damnable, and every now and then she used to hit them a Rap with her Stick, and so the Lads would have the Head-ach, or a Pain in the Bones for a Week, and this was all Witchcraft; Mother *Martyn*, or one of her Imps had bewitched them. If any one was taken with a Vomiting or Looseness, it was Mother *Martyn* still, and Curses upon Curses were thrown upon her for many Years.

Now it happened one Morning that the 'Squire came towards her House with his Pack of Hounds, and not being able to find a Hare, asked the old Woman's Advice as the sat spinning at her Door; Sir, quoth the old Woman, go to yon Hill and you will find that which will lead you a Dance. Away goes the 'Squire, and as she said he started a bouncing Puss, that led him many a dirty Mile, and was lost at last: In his Return home, Mother *Martyn* was sitting at her door spinning all in a Sweat: You have found me Sport (says the 'Squire), but d—n your Sport, since it has made me so faint that I can hardly sit my Horse, having some Thoughts that she had been the Hare that had led him such a Dance. Your Worship (says she) may drink a Glass of my Cordial Water if you please, it is good of the sort: And when he had drank it, Now (says she) take care of your Back-side between this and Home. Then the 'Squire rode away without giving her anything for her Favour; but before he came home was taken with a sharp griping Pain, which made him sh—t Pins and Needles, as he thought, and the belt Physician there about could not set him to rights in a Fortnight. The next Quarter Sessions he takes up Gammer *Martyn*, and without a long Process, had her burnt, as the Law directed them for Witches. For (says he) though she gave me Diversion in the Chase, she certainly bewitched me with her Spirit of Arse-Smart; she is plainly a Witch, for every Body has sworn their ill Healths proceeded from Mother *Martyn*'s Sorcery; and besides she was an old Woman.——It had also been said of her, that she was once seen walking in the shape of a Cat upon the Ridge of a House; and more over the hid a Mole under her Left Breast; and burnt the was by the common Hangman.—But if I may add one Thing more before I end her Story, which I had from a near Neighbour of her's, the chief Occasion of her Death was, that she and the 'Squire's Steward had not set their Horses together for some Years, and the Steward then set her out for Watch, and for a few Pence easily drew a Mob of Boys after her, whenever she came up to Town: The Witch is coming, says one; Here is Mother Damnable, says another: And so her Character became such, that the old Proverb was made good, *Some may better steal a Horse than another look ever an hedge.*

It is to be noted that the old Woman might, without being a Witch, tell the 'Squire where he might find a Hare, and might change Countenance, or appear in a Flutter when the 'Squire stopped at her Door, thinking her Dispute with the Steward had put the Squire into a Passion, and to make up the Difference might offer him a Dram, which most old Women have by them; and to bid him take care of his Backside, might only proceed from her unpolished Way of Thinking; and the Sharpness of his Stools might only happen from the Temper of his Body at that Time, as many People meet with frequently. I suppose from such reasonable Ways of Thinking, Mother *White*, a reputed Witch of *Hertfordshire*, or *Essex*, was saved from the Flames by a late Judge.

But to shew you how easy it is to make a malignant Witch, that is, such a one as Mother *Martyn*, or the worst of Witches was ever deemed to be, I will first give you an Account of the Accomplishments required, and then tell you how to make one any Day in the Week.

To make one of the Witches of old Times, you must choode an old Woman, very hagged and very ill-natured; she will then be so cunning, that if she has any little Hoard by her of Money, or a few Apples in her Orchard that she does not care to lose, she presently gives out of her own accord, that she can set Charms or Spells upon all that would attempt to rob her. This by degrees makes all the young Men and Boys tremble as they pass by her House, and brings all the young Women in the Country about her to learn their Fortunes: Then she begins to talk of an Ointment the Devil has given her to conjure herself into a real Witch, and does not grudge to say she can ride many hundred Miles in a few Minutes upon her favourite Broom stick, to meet her beloved *Lucifer*, and with him to play at *Rantum Scantum* on a Bed of Nettles. When you find a Woman thus qualified, she is either fit to make a Witch or a Bawd; then if by good Luck she can learn, either from Mother *Bunch*'s Closet opened, or some learned Physician, how to make intoxicating Draughts, or such as may Torment the Belly, she becomes Mitress of her Business. A Wife may meet her Gallant at her House whenever he will, while a little Dose of her sleepy Cordial may be given to the Husband; and if he proves fractious, then some of the griping Dose follows, and pinches his Guts till he is sufficiently rewarded for his Complaints. On the Other Hand, if the young Men come to her with a similing Countenance, and cross her Hand with a Piece or Silver, she prefently finds an Opportunity to make their favourite Witches fly into their Arms; or by another Draught, if the good Mother will shame any Body in the Parish, for an Insult offered to her, she will make them laugh at every thing they see for twenty four Hours, and so the Witch's Hovel becomes a meeting House for the pretty longing Girls and the young Fellows in the Neighbourhood, and there is not one of them will declare any thing that happens at the Witch's House; for if they do, she will not fail of giving them either a Dose of Madness or of Sleep, or of Laughing or Gripes, just as the Maggot takes her in the Head. The pretty Girls are her Witches and her Charms, and with them the sets Spells upon the young Men. By this Cunning she will lead any one of her Familiars into a Wood, or under a Hedge, or, in short, where she commands; and he accounts *a Touch of the Wand is very enchanting.*

Now we may examine how the Devil an old Woman should take upon her to live by such odd Things? I can only answer that such odd Things bring in a great deal of Money; for every one of the Company pays something towards it, and then do you not think the Witch might live very well by it ? I pray you how did Mother *Needham* get her Bread? was it not by this Means? And is not Madam —— doing the same this Day, and Mrs. ——, and my Lady ——,and 'Squire ——, and Count——, and Sir ——; but they indeed Witchcraft it in *London*, where the People know the Lord knows what; and therefore such Meeting must be in Masquerade: I then desire to know what is the Difference between the Witches of the Town and Country; the Answer is very short, when we consider that the Witches in the Country who give their Minds to Catterwauling, are esteemed Cats, for all Whores are called Cats, and all the Catterwauling. Folks, either in Town or Country, whether in Cat Skin or Harlequin Dresses, are Cats; so that the Country as well as the *London* Ladies are all one in point of Kissing, when they are metamorphoted on such Occasions; and this is the Reason why Witches are said to transform themselves into Cats. But pretty Girls may take what Shape they please, they are Witches still, and will enchant Mankind, let them do what they will: All Males will come to the Lure of Female. But to give a Word or two more concerning the old sort of Witches or Bawds, I find at this very time of Day, there is a Clan of Witches in the Island of *Majorca*, who from good Testimony eat the Leaf of an Herb, which raises then to such a Pitch of Madness, as can only be paralled by the *French* Prophets, that were among us of very late Date; they will seem by their Talk to bein the Air, to meet the Devil, and will then converse with any Man as if the Devil was in them.

But we have a sort of Mother Witch, that is next to these which are the Coffee and Tea Throwers, to tell Peoples Fortunes; but whether the Fortune is to be decided by Coffee or Tea, depends chiefly upon the Humour of the Fortune Tellers: If it is on the Coffee Side, they must have their Learning from Gypsies or Egyptians, whence Learning once abounded, and Coffee has grown from the beginning of Time: But the Gypsies we see about the Streets are not altogether so wise; their Colour is of the true Walnut Shell Tinge, and their Wit altogether in picking of Pockets; they are all Counterfeits. I just know that there is a little Difference between the Goers about and the Stayers at-home: As for the commons Gypsies, they will steal Tankards, and as for the best of the Coffee-Throwers, I was at her House, and while the was gone to get some Coffee to perform the Ceremony, I pissed in her Shoe, which cost at least seven Shillings, and into the Coffee Pot likewise, which she knew nothing of: So that I conclude neither of these sort of Witches have any great Notion of Conjuration; unless Miss *Nancy* wants *Tom*, or Miss *Sally* wants *John*, and then no doubt they can make up the Difference between them if they are well paid for it, but the itinerant Witches, such as the Gypsies, tell Fortunes for a Penny, and the Home set Witches will have a Shilling at least for their Advice.

The nett *Witch Dealers*, are those which deal with the Gypsies, and take their Magic chiefly from letting up Pokers against a decaying Fire, or laying on a Fire Shovel over the same when it is almost out, whilst the latter take their Counsel from their Coffee Pot and their own Corjectures. It I may give my Opinion in the Case, I should suppose that the setting of Pokers against Fire, is much more ancient than the Use of Coffee; for the first has been ever since the Discovery of Coal Mines at *Newcastle upon Tyne*, and the Use of Coffee in England has not been above fifty-five Years.

As for the Mother Tea Witches, or such as presume throw Tea-Grounds, they must certainty, to establish the Fortunes of People, bring their Learning from *China*, where the Tea only grows; for it we were to use a Drug so commonly as Tea is used, and did not know the Use of it, why do we use it. One may venture to offersive Guineas Reward to any one who can lead the *Chinese* Language; for there is not at present any Person who can tell the least tittle of it in *England*. Therefore Chalk or Powder of Poet would do the same thing, and thin *Tea-Castings* can be of no Import or Signification; so that *Tea-Witches* have no Foundation for their Fortune-telling, unless by what I have said before of the bringing young Witches to their Mates, and

their procuring a Copulation; and then the Proverb is verified, *Cat after kind.*

I could here give you an Account of various
Sorts of diminutive Witches in *London*; such as
Semstresses, Milliners, &c. of the old Race; but
I conclude, that all the Witches for my Mind are
young Women, which I presume may be procured
at the above said Places. When the Devil couples
with Witches, they bring forth Toads and serpents,
as some great Authors tell us.

One may add that there was another sort of
Witch two or three Years ago, that could enchant
hundreds of Families into amaze about her Coney
Warren , I mean the Woman about *Guildford*, who
pretended to breed Rabbits every Day, from the
bare seeing a Rabbit cross the Way before her; and
to far did the manage the Matter, being a Women
of a large Capacity, that several large Rabbits were
seen to come from her Body by the Sect of Cun-
ny-peepers, and among the left, two of note, who
blazed about her Fame as fit to be Mattress of all
the Cony-Warrens in *England*, for they had peeped
and, felt the Case, and opened it so far to the Public, that there were many thousands about *London*
could not eat, a Rabbit for a Twelvemonth, and
many hundred Pounds were lost by the Poulterers
on account of that Commodity: But at length by
many Reasons in Philosophy, by two or three great
Conjurers, that the Woman was really Mother to a
vault Number of Rabbits that they saw born, and
tha the crossing of the Rabbit before her must be

the Reason of it; it was discovered that the whole was done by Euchantment, *i. e.* by Confederacy, for a Woman in League with her brought her every Day or Night, privately, a Parcel of young Buns or Rabbits which she hid in her Bed, and every now and then the put one into *Burrow*, and then would begin to grunt and roar like a Devil, till she was delivered of her Burthen; but as soon as this Cheat was found out, it was presently concluded that the was not of the Strain of the old Witches, nor quite of the new Witches Sort, and then Rabbits were eaten again. This was a Piece of Witchcraft above the common way, though there has been a Woman at *Hammersmith* who said she was possessed by the Devil, and got Money by it, *i. e.* her Mother did, which was the same thing as the Rabbits Mother did; but this like the other was discovered to be an Impostor, and suffered accordingly.

Of Wizards and Conjurers

The Conjurers in ancient Times were out of our Reach; they kept that Knowledge to themselves, but yet with that Knowledge would get more Money than any of our Moderns, except Mr. *Lun*, or the late Mr. *Fawkes*.

Dr. *Faustus* and Friar *Bacon* were two very

great Conjurers in their Time; these were Wizards, and played the Devil, as some Folks say, in the Days of Yore: Dr. *Faustus*, because he had the first Knowledge of Printing, took the Bible in Hand, which used then only to be written, at a great Expence, even at about twenty or thirty Pounds a Piece, which in those Times were then equal to ten times the Money in our Days. *Faustus* printed a large Number of them, and sold them in foreign Countries as well as his own, and even to the Value of the Manuscripts, by which he amassed a vast Fortune. At last his Printing was discovered, and then it was said he could eat Loads of Hay, had fiery Dragons stewed for his Breakfast, had fried Toads and broiled Serpents for Dinner, and by way of Desert would change Men's Noses into Bunches of Grapes, or Bunches of Grapes into Noses, which was the same thing.

He could do more than *Moor* of *Moor-Hall* when he flew the Dragon of *Wantley*; he could devour Loads ef Hay, when the Dragon of *Wantley* (as he was suited) could eat up Houses and made no more of them than if they had been Geese and Turkeies.

So they both according to my Sense of the Matter, who were Men of great Estates, eat up their Fortunes at any rate, not valuing Men, Women, or Children:

　　　　——They eat all,
　　　　And left none behind,

But some Stones, dear Jack,
That they could not crack,
Which on the Hills you'll find,

Faustus spent his Estate to gratify the Fools who came to his Observatory, where he drank plentifully with such sort of Folks, and was generous enough to give those who were curious the Things which stood him in a large Expence; at last he grew poor, and then the *Devil take him*, said every one, for nobody came near him; and that was the Devil, for it was said the Devil swallowed him up, as Mr. *Lun* has it at his House in *Covent-Garden*, where I have seen it: So that he was no true Wizard upon second Thoughts.

The Dragon of *Wantley* too, may be deemed a thing now-a-days which signifies nothing, but let me assure you, he was a Gentleman once of very good Fortune, he would drink hard it is true, till *Moor* of *Moor-Hall* got all his Estate by Mortgage or otherways; and so *Moor* of *Moor Hall* conquered the Dragon.

It is said that Men drink like Dragons in the North, and one of an extraordinary Nature at *Wantley* might be called the Dragon of the Place; and I suppose *Moor* of *Moor-Hall* his Estate in Mortgage, and then the Lawyers came in, and there was an end of the Matter.

Friar *Bacon* was another Conjurer of *Oxford*, who invented the Brazen Head; but his Man *Miles* was one of the Families of Sad-Dogs, for when the

Brazen Head had been made for a long Time at vast Labour and Expence, *Miles* being left to look after it while his Master slept, he never took care to call Friar *Bacon* when it spoke, and so the whole Scheme came to nothing, or else all *England* was to have been walled round with Brass.

It seems to me that Friar *Bacon* was an Alchymist, and one aiming at the Philosopher's Stone; and I assure you whoever can get at that Treature, may not only encompass *England* with Walls of Brass, but Walls of Gold. There have been several Men of good Substance lately employing themselves about it, with a Design of paving our Streets with Gold, and I was in great Hopes of it in the Year 1720, when all the Bubbles were on Foot; but then all fell to nothing, whoever got by the Bargain: And since these things have happened, I can have no great Faith in the Philosopher's Stone, yet should like well enough to treat with such as could contrive to bring in the Cole plentifully.

A merry Fellow says that, Friar Bacon's Head, immediately before it burst to Pieces, foretold that the Brass Guns of our Navy were the Brass Walls he designed for us. In a Word, though we have not the the first, we have the last, and no Nation dare attack us; our Fleets can always protect us: "These, (says he) being given to shattering, may proceed from the shattered Brazen Head of Friar *Bacon*; read his History, and see farther. Another Man of Assurance says, "That the *English* are such brazen-faced Mortals ever since Friar *Bacon*'s Time, that they will face the whole World."

It is a Proverb that *two Heads are better than one*, and then to be sure if we were to lay our Heads together, as we have done in some late Wars, the folks who are our Enemies would find it so, that is as good as a Wall of Brass, only consisting of broken Parts, as other Walls do.

Or may we think that the Brazen Head of Friar *Bacon*, when he designed it, did not mean, as some would suggest, that a whole Head is better than a broken one; by which I understand, That to be all of one Mind would be much better than to be divided. But then, says another, Remember the Proverb, *Many Men, many Minds*; which, in my Opinion, must ever be, because they are naturally so; and if we are all of one Mind, we should become a Parcel of *Momes*, and have nothing to say to one another though some inconsiderate Fellows answer, You know nothing of the Matter, you love *Sukey Larkın*; so do I, say they then, Are we not all of one Mind? No, they reply presently, d—n you, you shall not have her to yourself, we will have her: and then they begin to battle it with me; then I desire to know whether we are all of one Mind.

But I must tell you how this great Conjurer, Friar *Bacon* has gone beyond the Lengths of the Wisdom I have been speaking of; for in a Penny Book I have of him, it is said, when King *Edward* the Third sent for him to Court, he was Conjurer

33

enough to bring a Cook Maid with a Spit, and a Shoulder of Mutton on it, from an hundred Miles distance, before the King, on purpose to confront her with one of the King's Servants, who had lain with her. And this I suppose is true, because it is in Print; but then Friar *Bacon* was so kind as to send her back again immediately about her Business, or else the Shoulder of Mutton might have been spoiled, the Master expecting it at a set Time, or the might have taken another Touch, and that might possibly have broken the Enchantment.

These are the old Heroes in Magick, and next to them. I place Mr. *Fawkes*, one of our modern Conjurers, who, after having anointed himself with the Sense of the People, became so great a Conjurer, that he amassed several thousand Pounds to himself: He was so celebrated a Magician, that either by the Force of his Hocus Pocus Powder, or by the Influence of his Conjuring Wand, he could presently assemble a Multitude of People together, to admire he Phantoms he railed before them, *viz.* Trees to bear Fruit in an Instant, Fowls of all sorts, change Cards into Birds, give us Prospects of fine Places out of nothing, and a merry Jig without either a Fidler or a Piper; and moreover, to shew that Money was but a Trifle to him, with a Conjuring Bag that he had, would every now and then shower, down a Peck or two of Gold and Silver upon his Table; and that this Money should not die with him, he has conjured up a Son who can do the same Things; so that one may say his Conjuration is hereditary.

* * *

But we must not forget Dr. *Partridge*, the Al-manack maker, Student, in Physick, Astrology, and Shoe-making; he could tell Fortunes, make Daffey's Elixir, gild Pills, and calculate Nativities, or mend Shoes, i. e. he could cure a bad *Sole*, but now, alas! his All (*Awl*) is at an *End* at *Last*, and they say he *waked* very rich before he died.

One Thing is memorable of him, which is, that he Could make Witches as appears from the fol-lowing Story. Once upon a Day an old Woman, who was of such Temper that he was continually snarl-ing at her Neighbours, and found that her Curse had no effect upon them, came to him in great Agony, saying, Good Doctor, I want your Help, I hate all the Word, and would tend them all to the Devil if I could; I have curst, and curst, and curst again, and fill my Neighbours live in quiet; but I have heard a Witch may do what the pleases, and Torment Folks by Peacemeals, till the fends them to the Devil; so, dear Doctor, make me a Witch if you can, and I will give you five Guineas. The Doc-tor you may be sure insisted upon ten, but rather than fail, finding the Woman would give no more Money, Mitress (says he, with his Spectacles on) lay down your Money, and you may come to me tomorrow Morning for a Box of Ointment that will do your Business. The Woman dropped him a fine Courtsey, and was early enough the next Morning for her precious Box, which was ready for her, and like Lightning flew to her Abode, stripped, and rubbed the Unguent on the Places he had directed, as her Face, Hands, &c. but it proved of so bad Savour, that there turned immediately to the Doctor, curling as much as she dared do; but recollecting herself that he was looked upon to be a Conjurer, submitted as much as her Stomach would let her, and said, I believe it was a T——d you gave me to annoint me with: Why then Friend, says the Doctor, you are a Witch, for it is really so as you say and I deserve my Money.

The noted Lord Rochester, when he took upon him to play the Mountebank, among others that flocked about his Stage, an honest Fellow came to him, that he was so much addicted to Lying, that he had not, nor could not speak one Word of Truth. Come to me To-morrow, says the Mountebank, and I'll make you speak Truth as soon I have you under my Hand; the next Day, the Man being naturally of an honest Temper, went early to get a Cure for that which some Folks would not be Cured of for all the World, *viz.* His Lordship take him on the Stage, bid him open his Mouth, and rubbed his Gums with a Sirreverence: By G—d, says the Man, this is a T—d. Why then by God says my Lord, you have spoke Truth, and I have cured your Distemper.

There are many more pretended Conjurers in the World, but beware of Counterfeits, you will find those have no Foundation of their own to let up upon, and so when you force them to open their Minds, they will answer nothing, or nothing to the Purpose.

But if you would be let into the Secret of Conjuration and Astrology, I advise you to go to some
Cobler of Distinction, such as Partridge, Poor Rob-
in, or a Lawyer; then you may pick up Learning
till you will he sick on it, and perhaps be poisoned
into the Bargain; for most of these Star-gazers fell
Physic and Nonsense together: And so by way of
Conclusion I present you with a lively Figure of a
Conjurer in the beginning.

If a Conjuror has not Reason to support his Credit, then
he is obliged to shew a few Tricks to support himself and
bring in the Pence.

When a Devil is to be introduced, it should be
properly with a Thunder-Crack; and there is nothing more stinging to the Ear than the *Pulvus-Ful-*

minans or Thunder Powder, which is made of Tar-
tar, Sulpher and Nitre, but it must be close topped
in a Bottle as soon as it is made; you may have it at
the Chymist, or see the Receipt for making it in Dr.
Quincy's Book of Pharmacy.

The way of using it is, to put the Quantity of half
a Thimble full of the Powder into a Fire Shovel,
and make somebody, who knows nothing of the
Matter, set it over the Fire, and as soon as it melts
it gives an astonishing Crack, which will ring in
the Ears of the People near it two or three Days,
though it gives no Light or Flash like Gunpowder.
This was one of the Wizards or Conjurers Tricks,
and our Forefathers had it to frighten the Folks
about them; and whoever has this Secret, may set
up for a Devil or Witch in the Country. But if after
this Thunder you would make a Devil or a Ghost
appear, then take the following Method.

Phosphorus, which one may buy at Mr. *God-
frey's* Chymist in *Southampton-Street, Covent-
Garden*, is an excellent thing to represent the Appearance of any Object we desire, in Flames of Fire
in a dark Room, it is like a Crayon, so that you may
draw with it as with a Pencil to represent any Figure
you desire; and when the Candles are there you can
see nothing; but when all is dark you will presently
discover the Figure in Fire, and always in Motion,
unless sometimes it may perhaps blind or lose itself
for half Minute, as if it vanished, buy will then rise
again in the same Shape, and waver about as if it
had Life in it for some considerable Time.

Though this *Phosphorus* dear, a Man may make a Maid come into his Arms, if he can write or draw-well against a Wall with it, and afterwards it is ten to one whether she swears a Rape against him. *Phosphorus* is to be kept in Water or Spirits, or it will consume.

One may with *Phosphorus* light a Candle by a Glass of *i. e.* cut off a Piece of it as big as a large Pin's Head, and stick it on the side of a large Glass of Water; mark the Place and then take any Candle in the Room and turn it downwards, and drip it out till no Fire is seen, and then while the Wick is hot, hold that to the Place where the *Phosporus* is put, and it will light in Streams of Fire in a blue Flame, such as Ghosts and Farts make.

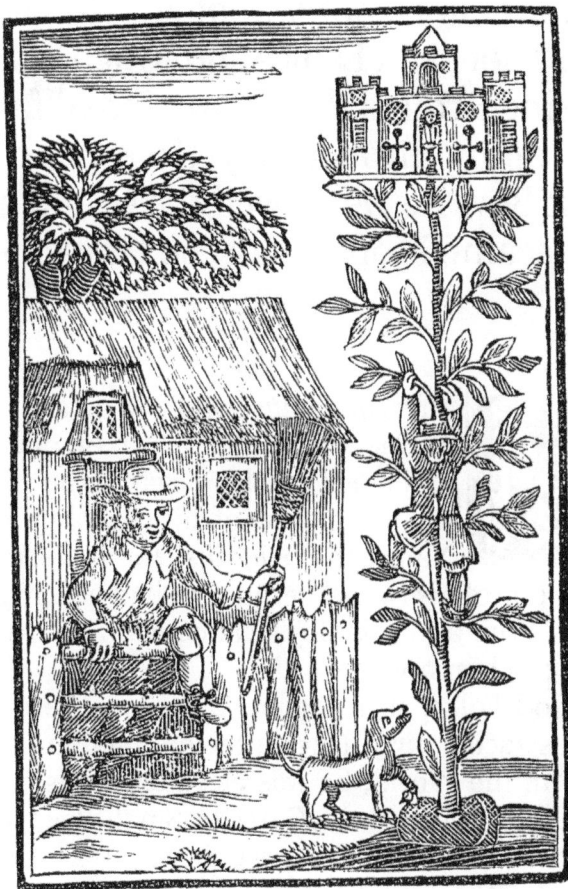

IV

Enchantment Demonstrated, in
the Story of *Jack Spriggins* and the
Enchanted Bean; Giving a Particular
Account of Jack's Arrival at the Castle

of the Giant *Gogmagog*; His Rescuing Ten Thousand Ladies and Knights from Being Broiled the Giant's Breakfast, Jumping through Key-Holes; and at Last Bow Be Destroyed the Giant, and Became Monarch of the Universe

affer *Spriggins*, who was an acute old Farmer, who could leer of one Eye and crack a Joke, began to tell about a comical Lad of his Family, of the Name of *Spriggins*, for he admired every one of his Name, because he had no Children of his own; and this Boy's Name was *Jack*, as we shall call him now.

Good Folks, says Gaffer *Spriggins*, there never was such a dirty, lazy, tatter-de-mallion Dog as *Jack* in the World; he was elevated in his Garret o' Nights, and had the Curse of Small Beer in his Kitchen o' Days, with an old Enchantress for his Grandmother and Companions. When I mention this Apartment, I ought in justice to let you know that the House was no more than a Hovel of a Cottage; it consisted but of two Rooms, if we may call them so, for really the Upper Apartment, which was the next Story to the Ground Floor, was next to the Thatch, in which Place he had often the Ben-

42

efit of Contemplation; for though he was a smart
large Boy, his Grandmother and he laid together, and between whiles the good old Woman in-
tructed *Jack* in many things, and among the rest,
Jack (says she) as you are a confortable Bed-fellow
I must tell you I have a Bean in my House which
will make your Fortune; you shall be richer than
an Emperor, you all have the whole World at your
Command; and as you now grow strong and lusty,
I design to give it thee one Day or other. Oh! says
Jack, dear Grandmother give me now that Bean,
that I may try how rich I can be, and then how
much I can love my dear Grandmother! No, Child,
says she, should I do that, you would grow rich
and turn Rake, and you would never think of your
poor Grandmother again: But, Sirah, says she, if I
was to know you would play such Tricks, I would
whip your little Narsey-parsey for you. Nay, says
Jack, Grandmother, don't hurt me. No, answers
the Grandmother, you lusty Boy, you know I love
you too well to hurt yous as I love you as becomes
me, and you ought to take Notice on't; and to *Jack*
made no Words about the Matter.

In the Morning as *Jack* was making his Grandmother Fire, Puss scratching among the Ashes
clawed out the Enchanted Bean, which his Grandmother had dropped out of her Purse by accident.
Odds Budd, says *Jack*, I'll set it in our Garden, and
see what it will come to, for I always loved Beans and
Bacon; and then what was wonderful! the Bean was
no sooner put into the Ground, but the Sprout of it

jumped out of the Earth, and grew so quick that it gave *Jack* a Fillip on the Nose, and made him bleed furiously: In he runs to his Grandmother, crying out, Dear Grandmother, save me, I am killed: No, says she, I now have only Time to tell you my Enchantment will be broke in an Hour's Time, I know it, you have got my Bean, and this Impertinence of your's will occasion my being transformed; yet if I am able I will sufficiently thrash your Jacket: But away runs *Jack*, and up the Bean he climbs, and the old Woman after him, with the Birch Broom in her Hands. The Bean was then about a Mile high, and by that Time he got at it, *Jack* was straddled up near half a Mile; and through her Vengeance and Ill-nature, not being able to reach the Boy, she fell down in a Fit for a Time, and as soon as her Hour was out, was turned into a monstrous Toad, and crawled into some neighbouring Mud or Cellar, in her way to the Shades: But *Jack* went on his Gallop, though the Bean grew more than a Mile an Hour, In truth the Bean grew forty Miles high, and while it was growing, some little Towns were built upon the Leaves as he went up, for him to refresh himself at: He called at one for a Pot of Ale, at another for Bread and Cheese, and at another, which was near the Giant's Castle, for what he could get, this had a very promising Aspect, for the Sign was as big as any on Ludgate-Hill: Here he thought to rest for a Time, and goes in strutting like a Crow in a Gutter: What have you to eat Landlord, says he; Every thing in the World, Sir, says the Landlord:

Why then, says *Jack*, give me a Neck of Mutton and Broth: Alas, says the Landlord, to-morrow is Market Day, how unfortunate it is! I cannot get you a Neck of Mutton to-night if it was to save my Soul: Well then get me something else, says *Jack*; Have you any Veal? No, indeed, Sir, not at present; but there is fine Calf fatting at Mr. *Jenkinson*'s, that will be killed on Saturday next: But have you any Beef in your House, says *Jack*? Why truly, Sir, says the Landlord, if you had been here on Monday last, I believe, though I say it that should not say it, you never saw so fine a Sir-Loin of Beef as we had, and Plum Pudding too, which the Justices who dined here, and their Clerks and Constables entirely demolished; and though I got nothing by them, yet their Company was a Credit to my House? Zounds, says *Jack*, have you nothing in the House? I am hungry, I am starving; but I hear a Cock crow, and from thence I am sure you have some Poultry, kill one of them and broil it: Yes, Sir, says the Landlord, but that Cock is the Squire's, he would not take forty Guineas for it. Well then, replied *Jack*, you may kill a Hen or a Chicken. O Lord, Sir, I have no Chickens, answered the Landlord, and the two Hens that I have belong to the Game Cock, and they have incubated as I may say, their Eggs a Fortnight; but I believe we shall have Chickens a Week hence. Have you no Eggs in the House? says *Jack*. No, Sir, indeed, answers the Landlord, but Nest Eggs, which we make of Chalk. Why then, says *Jack*, what the Devil have you got? Why to tell you the Truth, Sir, I don't know that I have anything in the House to eat; for the 'Squire and his Huntsmen called here this Morning and devoured what we had, all our Bacon, all our Cheese, and all our Bread; but I could have got you some nne Trouts from the Miller's only a little Time before you came in he sent all his Fish up to Sir *John's*. Why then, 2ays *Jack*, I find I must go to Bed Supperless. Aye Master, answers the Host. Then give me some Drink says *Jack*. That I can do, for I have just brewed; and if you love new Drink, I can fit you to a tittle, for it has not been in the Tun half an Hour.

Thus was poor *Jack* plagued by the Enchantment of his Grandmother, who was resolved to lay him under her ill Tongue, so long as her Power lasted. But just as he fell in with this starving Prospect, off goes the Top of the House, the Host was turned into a beautiful Lady; and in pops a dozen pretty Youths, dressed like Pages in green Satin, laced with Silver, and white Feathers in their Caps, each of them mounted upon a Hobby Horse, finely bedecked with Ribbons, Tinsel, and Feathers; and in full Chorus most harmoniously addressed themselves to *Jack*, saluting him with the Titles of Sovereign Lord of the Manor, and invincible Champion: 'Tis this Instant that your supposed Grandmother the Queen of Pomonkey has taken her Passage to the Shades, her Enchantment is broke, and we bring you the full Power of possessing all the Pleasures you desire:

The fair Lady that stands before you is Empress of the Mountains of the Moon: young as she seems to be, was your Grandmother's Black Cat, and by Enchantment has worn that Shape four hundred Years: It was he that put it in your Mind to plant this wonderful Bean by scratching in the Ashes, and the is now entirely at your Highness's Disposal whether the hall live or die: You have a thousand *Jack Catches* now attending you without, with Alters and Hatchets to make an End of her, when your Honour pleases to direct her Execution; or else you have a fiery Dragon gaping for her, if you give but once the Signal for her Death: This Box, great Sir, bears you the absolute Power over her, over us, over old Scratch, or *Nicholas* the Antient. Your Grandmother, illustrious Sir, when she found the Loss of her Bean, and the Shortness of her Power, invoked an Assembly of Inquietudes to attend you, and so transformed this Miracle of Nature into the Host you have been talking with. Why in truth, says Jack, I thought it was a Woman by filling me so full of Expectation: But, Gentlemen, have you got any Bread and Cheese in your Pockets, for I am bloody hungry? But since it is all Enchantment, as I begin now to find by the Alteration of my Body, I feel sprinklings of generosity flow in my Veins for my Grandmother's dear Pussy, who has so often pur'd about me; I have Nobleness of Spirit to excuse my innocent Landlord, and Gratitude enough to take the fair Lady to my Arms.

It requires no more then, exalted Monarch, says the Pages, but to put on the Ring inclosed in that Box, and you will instantly possess five Wishes, and on the top of the Ring your Highness will find a Marble red Stone, given to your Grandmother by the King of *Strombolo*. If you are engaged in Combat, turn the Stone to the North, and you may conquer Giants, Dragons, and Basilicks and while you keep it to the South, you will flow in Plenty and enjoy everything else you desire.

Is that all you have to say? says *Jack*: Yes, and please your Honour, replied the Pages; and then put on the Ring; at which Moment the remaining Part of the Inn was changed with a terrible Crack into a delightful Summer House or Pavilion, where a Table was spread with the most elegant Dishes, and the Sideboard furnished with the richest Wines. This, says *Jack*, pleases me above all Things in the World; it is my first Wish completely: But then he espied his Lady to be stark naked: I wish, Madam, says *Jack*, you was as well cloathed as the greatest Queen in the World; when immediately the was adorned in the gayest Princely Robes. Now, says *Jack*, I wish for some good Music; and in an Instant down came a dozen or two of excellent Fidlers. He then wished them to play the Black Joke, and so they went on for an Hour, till he had cramed his Carcass. And for the fifth Wish he wished to be in Bed with his fine Lady; and as the Laws of Enchantment order it, a Wish is no sooner thought on but executed, so were our Couple enchanted into a Crimson Velvet Bed, embroidered with Gold and Pearls; the Room illuminated with an hundred Wax perfumed Lights placed in glass Sconces; the Orange Flowers, and the small ones made of mahogany and other fine Wood, adorned with Pyramids of Sweetmeats and refreshing Drams, from the true Barbadoes Citron to the humble Gin. Neither was there wanting a Chamber Pot on each Side of the Bed, and a Brace of Closestools in separate Closets, for fear of the worst, by which Convenience lay the Works of several eminent modern Authors, *by way of wipe.* I should have observed, that when the Princes was conjured into the wonderful Apartment, she was attended by twelve Damsels cloathed in silver, who knew to her Assistance mounted upon as many Rose-buds: These were followed by an impudent Shoe-bay, whose Business it was to clean her Ladyship's Shoes again the Morning. So that there was nothing wanting to complete the Happiness of the illustrious Couple. In short the Attendants withdrew, and we leave them now to play their Rantum-scantum Tricks till the next Mornings. I may add, that *Jack* had so much Business upon his Hands that Night, that he fell asleep in the Morning, and dreamt a Dream, in which the Patroness of the Enchantment appeared to him; and after having touched him and his Princess three Times with a Wand, struck out of their Memories all Thoughts of what they had been, and, consumed them in Princely Graces: Then whisking her Wand three Times over her Head, whispered Prince *John* of his Progress to the Top of his Bean, and how he should come to the Castle of Giant *Gogmagog*, by whom himself and his Princess should be favourably received, and entertained three Days without Danger, but he must be sure to keep the Stone in his Ring inclining to the North, and his Princess on his North Side, that then he should be in seeming Danger of his Life as well as his Princess; but by turning the Stone of his Ring under the Bent of his Finger, the Princess should immediately change into a Basilisk and kill all that were within reach of her Eyes except himself, and then as soon he could assure himself of Safety it was only to turn up his Ring as it had been before, and then the Princess would resume her Shape, and he become! Master of the Giant's Treasure. In the mean times the placed an enchanted Fly upon the Princess's left Breast to convey her as a Flying Horse would do, when the happened to be weary with climbing, and to departed.

Then Prince *John* began to rub his Eyes, and stretching himself with a Yawn or two, turned to his dear Prince's, who just waked from the same Dream he himself had; there was the Fly upon the Breast of the Lady, which they carefully took off and put into a little gold Cage, which they found placed on a Table by them, and after a merry Turn or two, they disposed themselves for getting up, and were immediately attended with Pages and Virgins. They had a delightful Breakfast, were dressed sumptuously, and set out for a Walk towards the Castle, the Pages leading their Hobby horses in their Hands, with one of an extraordinary Kind and Workmanship; for the Prince and the Virgins had each hold of their Rosebuds; and as for the Princess's enchanted Fly, the had hung it in its Cage, to the Chain of her Watch. It happened that the Company by means of the enchanted Air, had got Appetites like Horses, and by agreement the Prince and Princess set down under the Side of a Hill covered with Orange Trees and Myrtles, the Banks adorned with Cowslips, Primroses, Hyacinths, and Violets; before them was a purling Stream, and the Woods resounded with the harmonious Notes of Nightingales, Linnets, Canary, and other Singing Birds, when on a gentle Breeze was wasted an hundred Cupids, each bearing a Salver of Gold furnished with the richest and most delicate Meats; while on the other Hand; the Trouts, Salmons, Carp, and other Inhabitants of the Stream leaped upon the Banks, with a proper Supply of Nectar, Ambrosia, Burgundy, Champaign, Hermitage, Frontigniac, and Tokay, Wines, not forgetting a Dram or two for the Virgins of Honour.

The Prince and Princess were delightfully regaled, whilst the Zephyrs attended them with refreshing Air; and when their Company had satisfied themselves, the Remainder of the Entertainment vanished: And as it is not proper to walk muck after a hearty Repast, the Prince judged it convenient to ride the rest of the Way towards the Castle.

And now no sooner was the Fly let out of its Cage, but itself and all the Hobby-horses and Rose-buds were changed into Palfreys, adorned with the richest Trappings, and away they go in the grandest Manner, passing by many Knights and Ladies, and were informed that there were many before them, when, on a sudden they heard a Voice cry out (for they could hear many Miles farther than any one else)

> Fee-Faw-Fum
> I smell the Blood of an *English-Man*;
> Whether he be alive or dead,
> I'll grind his Bones to make my Bread.

But this did not trouble, either the Prince or his Lady or Attendants; they all knew they had safety enough in their Hands, and galloped on 'till they arrived at the Castle of Wonders, when they soon espied the Giant *Goginagog*, who was picking his Teeth with a great Tree pick Case was such another Thing as the Monument in His Tooth *London*; he had a Bowl of Punch as big as St. *Paul*'s Church, and the Cup that he drank out of was about the Size of the Dome of St. *Paul*'s; for his Tobacco Pipe he had the exact Model of the Pyramidical Building near the Water-side in *Southwark*, where the damaged Tobacco is burnt; and his Tobacco Stopper was like the Water Engine belonging to the York Buildings Company; and his Tobacco-Box was about the

Size of Westminster Hall: But, however, he sake up when the Prince and his Retinue appeared, and saluted them, bid them welcome, and offered them the best Entertainment he could give them, whilst the Prince for Safety's sake turned the Stone of his tro the North; for he had never seen so huge a Man before.

They were introduced into the Castle through the richest Apartments immaginable; and what was extraordinary, the great Giant shrunk into a common Size, and appeared like other Men. The Furniture was vastly rich, the Attendants without Number, and the Equipage magnificent, and nothing was wanting entertain our illustrious Couple with splendour befitting their Rank. The Gardens were splendid as those at Versailles, the Parks of vast extent, and, in a Word, so well furnished with all sorts of Game, that no other could parallel them, which pleased the young Couple extreamly, knowing full well they would be soon at their own Disposal.

But they had now passed near the three Days with the Giant, who grew desperately in Love with the Prince is, and resolved to have her at any Rate, even at the Expence of Devouring her Husband; which he could have done at a Mouthful well enough, if he had been a common Man. But Enchantment is a great Help to Men in such Distress, and the Prince and his Lady went to Bed well satisfied: They were no sooner laid down on their Pillow, but they heard a mighty Sobbing and

Mourning of many Virgins, fighing and grieving at their hard Fortunes, that the Giant was to make a Breakfast of them the next Morning.

Now you must know, the Stone in the Prince's Ring being turned to the South, he could see and know what the pleased and having consulted with the Princess about the Destruction of the Giant, My Dear, (says he) shall I make the Proof of changing you into a Cockatrice or Basilisk for there is a Mouse in the Room, and if your Looks kill that Animal we shall be sure of the rest, for it may be *multum in parvo*. The Experiment was made in an Instant, and the Princess her Eyes and whole Body, became so bright, that it was even dazling to her Husband; and the Mouse no sooner beheld her, but burst with a prodigious Crack: Then the Ring was turned again, and all Withes were in the Prince's Power; he immediately slipt through the Key Holes of Doors and young Ladies we large Gallery, where narrow Crannies till he came to a large Gallery, where several thousand young Ladies were tied up like Calves o'fatting, and be moaning theirhard Case, Alas! dear Prince, (says they) to-morrow early shall we be broiled and crushed between the Giant *Gogmagog*'s monstrous Teeth, if you do not save us; and there are ten thousand Knights below in as bad a Condition. You are then all safe, (says the Prince) for the Giant will be destroyed as soon as the Sun rises, and I fall then take possession of my Dominions.

He had no sooner said this, but he released the Ladies from their Bridles, and summoned the

Princess's Virgins to attend them with such Necessaries as they wanted. Then he whisked through the Cracks and Key Holes, till he reached the Place where the Knights were confined, and they like the Ladies were tied up to their good Behaviour, and were moreover restrained, the Use of their Hands, which he soon, changed to their Satisfaction, and gave them the Assistance of his Pages, with the Promise to release them the next morning. Then were the Rooms where these Prisoners of bath Sexes were kept, illuminated, and furnished with every refreshing Liquor while the Prince returned to his Lady, and related what had past.

The Day no sooner broke, but up got the Prince and Princess, and walking, into a Bower refreshed themselves with some Fruits, and the Giant appeared with a Sword in his Hand, says he with a hoarse Voice, Thou Prince of Pitty, this Moment you die, and the next Instant will I solace myself in the Delights of thy Princess. The Prince and Princess immediately got from their Seats, and while the Prince was turning his Ring towards the North, the Giant hit him a Thundering Stroke with his Sword; but he night as well have hit a Rock of Diamonds as wound the Prince; for by this Time the Ring was in a proper Station, and the Princess was changed into a Cockatrice or Basilisk. The Giant at this gave a great Groan, fell on his Knees, trembled, and fell down dead: Then there was a great Shout in the Castle, the Doors flew open, the Knights and Ladies Tallied forth to congratulate their Highnesses, and proclaim them, as their Sovereigns; they became their Vassals, and attended them in their delightful Palace and Royalty in the most perfect Happiness, And so far for Enchantment, which some old Women first set on foot to amuse Children, and is now finished by the Author, with no other View but to assure his Readers that Enchantment proceeds from nothing but the Chit Chat of an old Nurse, or the Maggots in a Madman's Brain.

V

Of Spectres, Ghosts, and Apparitions; the Great Conveniences Arising from Them, and How to Make Them

hen the Men and the Maids have end-
ed their Gambols, are all seated about
the Fire, and Bed Time is drawing on,
then *John* begins some dismal Story to
the Company about Apparitions and
Hobgoblins, and so about it goes till all the rest of
the Society are drawn into the same kindy of Dis-

course, and frightened out of their Wits with dreadful Apprehentions: A Mouse cannot stir, but *Nan* creeps close to *John*; *Sue* hugs *Tom*, and none dare lie alone; then Love and the Devil couples them together, and each one has a Mate for that Night; and when the Thing is once done, there is very little Ceremony used afterwards, whenever a proper Opportunity offers between the Parties, and ten to one but the Parish is filled with Bastards nine Months after, unless the pregnant Maidens make their way to *London* in time, and top their Kids upon some smug Apprentices by such Means they get a spell of Money deck themselve's forth, renew their Maidenheads, and either set up an Alehouse with the Mon that their Fear debauched, or else change the End of the Town, get ace quainted with some eminent Bawd, and for are made the Fandlings of some raking Coxcomb's Fortune for a while, and then turned off to walk the Streets. If it happens this way, then the Story of the Sprite was a dismal Story indeed for the forsaking of the first true Love, may bring the Ballad of *Bateman* before them; where they may plainly see in the Picture, that the Devil flies away with such false Wretches. But I have more Compassion for a tender hearted Maiden, than to think that where a Sixpence has once been crooked between her and her Sweetheart, he and ever forsake him, especially if he has any Notion of the Devil's Claws and forked Tongue, or the direful Horrors she must be subject to from the Hauntings of Ghosts and Spectres, whenever the happens to be alone after

Candlelight; then may the expect to see the Candle burn blue, the Chairs gallop about the Room, be tuned with Shrieks and Groans from every Quarter of the Room, when with a hideous Roar enters a ghastly Figure in a winding Sheet, with a lighted Taper in one Hand, and a bloody Dagger in the other, crying out for revenge, and talking up to you with long Strides, and great Saucer Eyes, rattling of Chains; and a Cloven Foot. This I am sure would be enough to frighten the stoutest Man that ever wore a Head, much more Women, who are made of such tender Stuff.

But there are many Ballads and History Book sold in *Moor-Fields*, which relate the many dreadful Ends that un constant Lovers have come to, as well as in Dr. *Glenville*'s great Book of Ghosts and Apparitions, where you may soon find these Assertions confirmed, and see these Spectres set in a true Light; but the Doctor's Book: indeed is too I high Priced for every one to purchase, and a Ghost is not to be seen every Day about *London*, unless opes was to pay for it at one of the Play Houses, and that would cost as much as the Book. Nor must you expect a Ghost to appear *gratis* in *Hand-Alley*, as it did seven Years ago, as thousands can testify, for that was laid for ninety-nine Years in the Red Sea by the Rev. Mr. M——— and the learned Dr. H———.

I only tell you of these Things that you may be fully apprised how dreadful a thing a Ghost is, and what a wretched Case you must be in, if you are once haunted by a Ghost of your own making, that is, if you was to break your true Love's Heart by Inconstancy, or make him hang or drown himself, or make him cut his Throat from Ear to Ear, for your Breach of Faith to him.

But doubtless you will say, after this long Harangue, why does not the Author give us a Story or two of some frightful Spectre for us to talk about when we have a Mind to frighten one another into a Love-fit, or preserve a constant Love between us: To this the Author answers, so he will, and you shall have them of two or three sorts.

Of a terrible Ghost

There is a melancholy Narrative in the Ballad of *Bateman*, expressing the horrible Circumstances of a Lady's being carried away by the Ghost of her true Love, who had hanged himself for her Inconstancy. Read the Ballad and tremble: but much more tremble at the following Story.

Mr. *Thomas Stringer*, a Gentleman of good Fortune, courted the greatest Beauty in his Country, who received all his Addresses with the fondest Love and Affection that could be; he seemed to be the Man for her Money, and a Piece of Gold was bent between them, as a sacred Pledge of their mutual Affections. But there were many more Lovers that followed her daily, and by bad Luck one of them, by some way or other gained her Affections, and got to Bed to her. In the Mean while *Stringer* had Intelligence of it, and no wand then upbraided her of Infidelity: But she in a gallant way returned, that she would do what she would with her own if she thought fit, and keep what Company the pleased: This Answer stuck in *Stringer*'s Stomach for a few Days, till he was certified of her being false to her Vow, not only in lying with one Man, but was well satisfied the received the Addresses of many, and so poisoned himself.

But a few Nights after, what a terrible Figure did he so poisoned himself make in her Bed Chamber! his Hair was nothing but Serpents, his Lilly-white Hands and his pretty little Feet were become like Eagles Claws, he crawled like a Toad along the Floor, croaking as he went, and glaring Eyes withs Horror in their Looks; he had a Light all about him, as if he was red hot. The Lady was all affrighted at his ghastly Appearance, and then hugged and pulled her Garllant, and by no Means could he awake him, while the Toad-shaped Creature was crawling up the Bed, and them kissing her with his ugly Mouth, spit Venom in her Face, and in a hideous Voice hallooed out, Now I have caught the faithless B——h, and will be revenged of the vile con founded Strumpet: After which the Ghost with his iron Clawstore herto Pieces, and sent her Scraps to the Devil, as a just Reward for her Treachery. All the while this was doing, the Candle, which stood on the Table, burnt Blue, which gives me Room to think that a Ghost and a Fart are the same Thing, for a Fartwill make the Candle burn Blue as well asa Ghost.—— And then I awaked, and cuddled close to my Bed-fellow.

Another Story of a Ghost; and how far it concerned Bishop

Dr. *Glanville*, famous for a Book of Witches and Apparations, was once selling a certain Bishop of their dreadful Effects, and begged his Lordships Opinion thereon: Indeed, says my Lord, I have often heard of such Things, and was once surprised myself about one o'Clock in the Morning, I heard something—Pray go on, my Lord, says the Doctor; but what did you hear? Why, replies my Lord, I heard a strange Noise on the Stairs, coming Lump, Lump, Lump, And pray what then? says the Doctor. Oh answers my Lord, and then with a great Thump my Chamber Door flew open. My good Lord, says the Doctor, I perceive you are of my Opinion: And then, continues his Lordship, I saw a tall Man enter my Room with a very grim Countenance. Nay then, says the Doctor, that must be a Ghost or the Devil And immediately, said the Bishop, my Chamber was enlightened, he stalked to the Side of my Bed, and drew the Curtains. Nay, says the Doctor, then it must be a Ghost: But had your Lordship Courage to speak to it? Yes, replies his Lordship, and I received a satisfactory Answer. Now, my Lord, says the Doctor, we are come to the Point; I find find now that your Lordship has a belief in such Things, though you have been pleased to banter me about my Thoughts of Apparitions. My Lord answered, Good Doctor, it is true, for it-was the Watchman, who finding my Street Door open, was seeking for somebody or other to shut it, and happened by mistake to come into my Room. So in the Picture Harlequin lights in the Ghost, for how the Devil do you think a Ghost can be in the dark; and if the Devil should stand at his Bed's-head, it is because he had said, *Get thee behind me Satan*, or *Avoid me Satan*: And therefore I sup-pose the Engraver only made the Devil peeping out behind the Bed.

But now I come to an extraordinary Case of an Apparition.

A Lad of my Acquaintance coming home late in Moon-shiny Night, just as he came to a Stile was terribly frightened at an Appearance which was very strange to him, such a thing as the com-mon Folks say, makes their Hair stand an end; he could not get over the Stile for the Blood of him, for he saw a black Man, at least forty Yards long, wagging his Head at him, but go home he must, or lie in a Ditch, where Ghost might come; and to make short of his Journey on so Desperate an Occasion, he went a little way about, and broke his way through a Quickiet Hedge, where he lost much Blood by the Scratches of the Thorns. When he came home you may be sure his Father or Mas-ter thrashed him heartily for hurting himself; but when their Passion was over they led the Youth to-wards the Phantom, that he might see what it was that gave him the Disturbance; and though loth to go, as he came nearer, holding fast by his Father and Mother, he began to discover that the frightful Ghost was not what heat first apprehended, and the nearer he came to it, still it varied from the first Appearance, till at last coming close to it, he found but it was only a tall Weed, waved a little by the Wind; and its Shade by the Moon-shine had cast a Figure on the Ground, which had almost frightened him out of his Wits. And if this Story does not prove that there are Ghosts, then I have no more to say.

VI

Of Fairies, Their Use and Dignity

M y Grandmother has often told me of Fairies dancing upon our Green, and that they were very little Creatures, cloathed in Green; they would do good to the industrious People, but they pinch the Sluts; they would steal Children, and give one of their own in the Room; and the

Moment any one saw them they were struck Blind of one Eye. All this I have heard, and my Grand Mother, who was a very tall Woman, said she had seen several of them, which I believe because she said so; the said moreover, that they lived under Ground, and that they generally came out of a Mole-hill; they had fine Music always among themselves, and danced in a Moon-shiny Night around, or in a Ring, as one may see at this Day upon every Common in England, where Mushrooms grow. But though my Grand mother told me so, it is not unlawful to enquire into a Sacret of this Nature, and so I spoke to several good Women about it.

When I asked one whether there was such a Things as Fairies, Aye, says she, I have seen many a Time: Another said, there's no room to doubt of it, for you may see thousands of their Rings upon our Common, &c.

I found, however, another way to be satisfied of the Matter, and heard the following Story of Fairies from a Person of Reputation.

A Gentlewoman and her Husband were going into the Country, and thought it best to retire out of Town four or five Miles the Night before, to receive the Stage Coach and avoid the Ceremony of taking leave of their Friends, which are generally more troublesome than welcome on that occasion, and being gone to Bed in a Country Town where Fairies walked, about Twelve o'Clock up comes a little Woman not much bigger than one's Thumb, and immediately follows a little Parson, also a

great Number of People, and a Midwife with a
Child in her Arms; and I suppose by their Power,
Chairs were set for them: But it happened they
wanted a Godmother for the Child, for it was to
be Christened that Night; so says the good Fairy,
Father, the Gentlewoman in the Room will do us
that Favour: Ay, says the rest of the Company, it is
a good Thought; and up brisked the Fairy Father to
the Bed-side, and called out the Lady, who did the
Office; for which the Father gave her a large Dia-
mond Ring. All this while the Lady's Husband was
as fast as a Church, and knew nothing of the Matter. But in the Morning, good lack, the Case was al-
tered; he espied the fine Ring upon his Wife's Finger; How came you by that, my Dear says he. Why,
my Love, replies she, the Fairies have been here
to-night, and told him the Story of the Christen
ing: Zounds, says he, the Ring is Sir *John*'s Ring;
I know the Stone: I have often seen Familiarities
between you and him, and now am convinced of
your Treachery, And so suppose he took his Wife
to be a Whore.

The Fairies were very necessary in Families, as
much as Bread, Salt, or Pepper, or any other such
Commodity, I believe; because they used to walk
in my Father's House, and if I can judge right of
the Matter, they were brought into all Families
by the Servants; for in old Times Folks used to go
to Bed at Nine o'Clock, and when the Master and
Mistress were lain on their Pillows, the Men and
Maids if they had a Game at Romps and blundered

up Stairs, or jumbled a Chair, the next Morning every one would swear it was the Fairies, and that they heard them stamping up and down Stairs all Night, crying, Waters locked, Waters locked, when there was no Water in any Pail in the Kitchen.

So from what I have said, the Hobgoblins, the Witches, the Conjurers, the Ghosts, and the Fairies, are not of any Value, or worth our Thought. And so I conclude with an Epilogue relating to Fairies.

Epilogue

I.

Come, follow, follow me,
Ye Fairy Elves that be,
Come follow me your Queen,
And trip it o'er the Green;
Hand in Hand we'll dance around,
For this Place is Fairy Ground.

II.

When Mortals are at rest,
And snoring in their Nest,
Unseen and unespied,
Through Key Holes we do glide;

Over Tables, Stools, and Shelves,
We trip it with our Fairy Elves.

III.

But if the House be foul,
With Platter, Dish, or Bowl,
Up Stairs we lightly creep,
And find the Sluts asleep;
There we pinch their Arms and Thighs,
None us hears, and none us espies.

IV.

But if the House be swept,
And from Uncleanness kept,
We praise the Household Maid,
And surely she is paid,
For each Morn before we go,
We drop a Tester in her Shoe.

V.

Upon a Mushroom Head
Our Table Cloth is spread;
Grain of Rye or Wheat
Is the Diet that we eat,
Pearly Drops of Dew we drink
In Acorn Cups up to the Brink,

VI.

But if our Diet fails,
The luscious Fat of Snails,
Between two Nut-shells stew'd,

Makes Meat that's easy chew'd
Brains of Worms, and Marrow of Mice
Make a Dish that's wondrous nice.

VII.

The Grashopper, Gnat, and Fly,
Serve for our Minstrels high;
Grace said, we dance awhile,
And so our Time beguile;
And when the Moon doth bide her Head,
The Glow-worm lights us home to Bed.

VIII.

O'er Tops of dewy Grass,
So lightly do we pass,
That the young and tender Stalk
Ne'er bends where we do walk,
Yet in the Morning may be seen
Where we the Night before have been.

FINIS

www.ingramcontent.com/pod-product-compliance
Lightning Source LLC
Chambersburg PA
CBHW031538260326

41914CB00039B/1998/J